DOWNEAST DAYDREAM

A Maine Coloring Vacation

TWIN FAWN MEDIA

TWIN FAWN MEDIA

Published by Twin Fawn Media
www.twinfawnmedia.com

Copyright © 2015 by Becky Chase

All rights reserved.
No part of this book may be reproduced in any form without the express written permission of the illustrator.

ISBN-13 978-0692555224
ISBN-10 0692555226

Cover design by Becky Chase.

Printed in the U.S.A.

DOWNEAST DAYDREAM

A Maine Coloring Vacation

BECKY CHASE

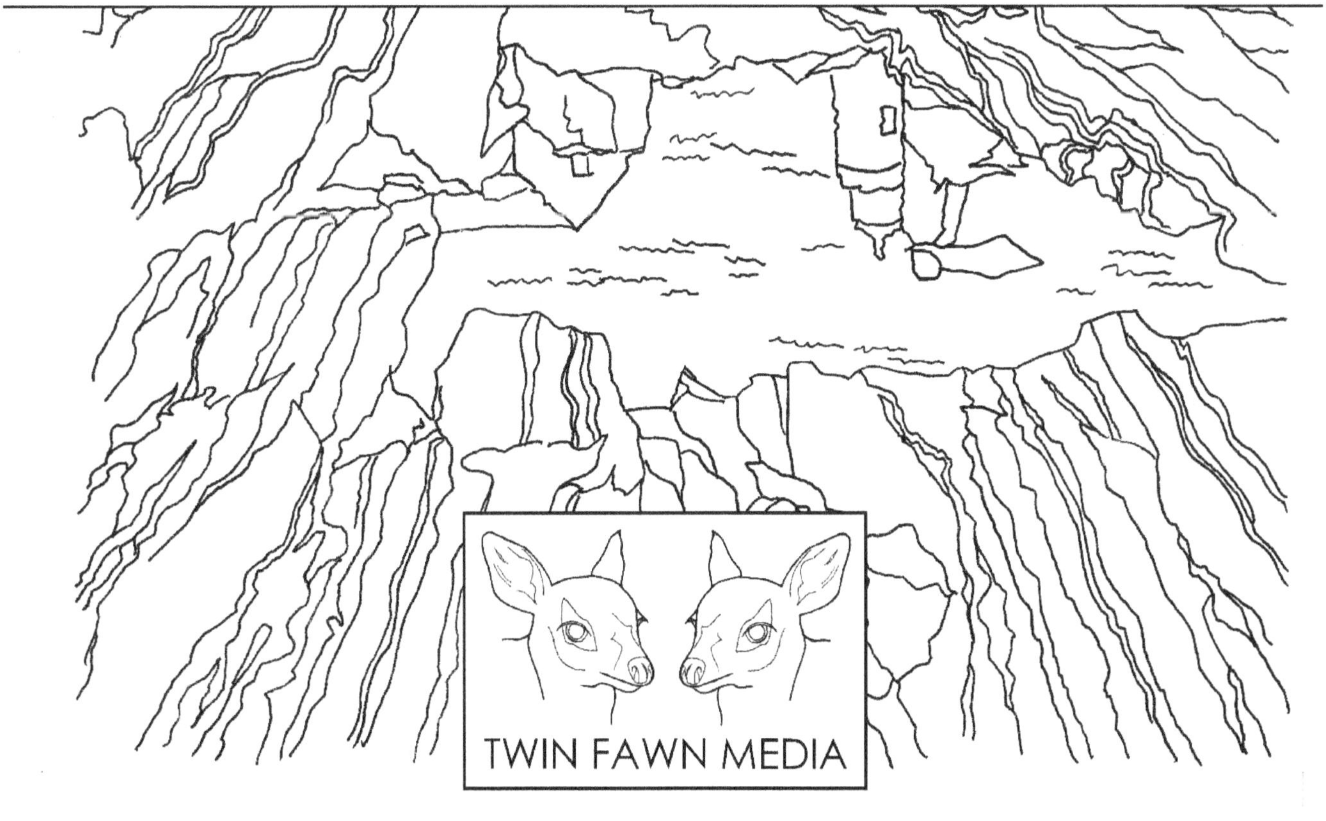

TWIN FAWN MEDIA

For my sister

KATHERINE CHASE HUBBARD

Who for some reason continues to give me colored pencils for Christmas every year

Though I never use them.

Table of Contents

State of Maine Song	1
Note on Color Application	2
Bass Harbor Head Light	3
Maine Boot	5
Seashells	7
Victoria Mansion	9
Chickadees	11
Bayberry	13
Whitehead Passage	15
Buoy Pattern	17
Lobster on Ocean Floor	19
Ski Slopes	21
Munjoy Hill	23
Twin Fawns	25
Widgery Wharf	27
Buoy Mandala	29
State of Maine Seal "Dirigo"	31
Wildflowers	33
Puffins	35
Pemaquid Point Light	37
More Seashells	39
Moose	41
Wild Blueberries	43
Harbor Seals	45
Lobster Pattern	47
Monarch Butterflies	49
Monhegan Island	51

Oh, Pine Tree State,

    Your woods, fields and hills,

Your lakes, streams and rock bound coast
    Will ever fill our hearts with thrills,

And tho' we seek far and wide
    Our search will be in vain,

To find a fairer spot on earth
    Than
        Maine!
            Maine!
                Maine!

        - Roger Vinton Snow, *State of Maine Song*

NOTE ON COLOR APPLICATION

Crayons, colored pencils, and marker pens can all be used on the drawings in this book.

If using marker pens, it may be worthwhile to place an extra sheet of paper behind a page in case of bleed-through.

Most importantly, have fun!

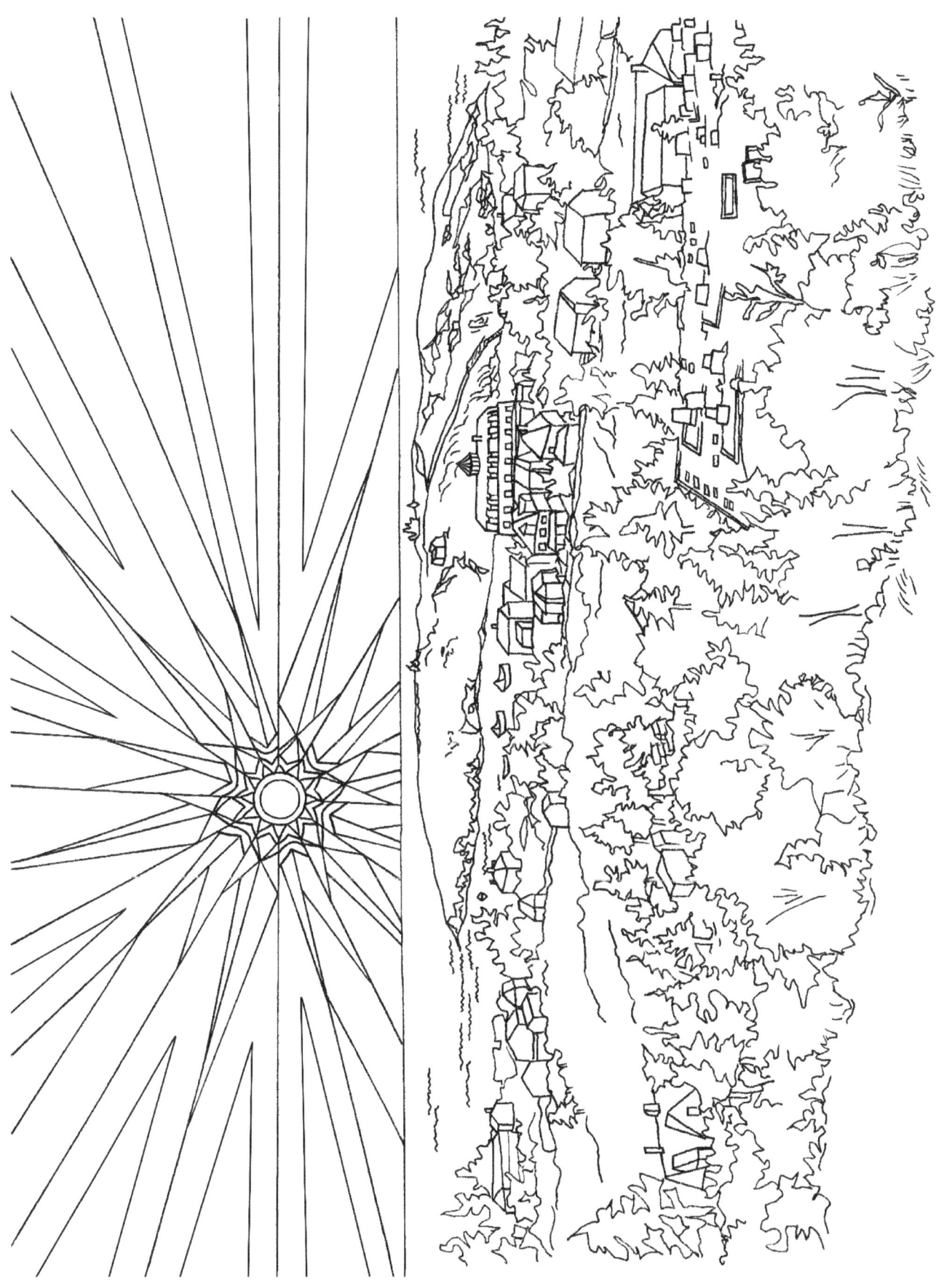

ABOUT THE ARTIST

Becky Chase was born and raised in Portland, Maine and grew up spending summers on an island in Casco Bay. She is a ninth-generation Mainer, with her sixth great-grandfather Ezekiel Bradford settling in Turner in 1782.

Though Becky has been creating art since childhood, her practice in line drawing began in 2011. To view more of her artwork, visit www.twinfawnmedia.com.